Clement Attlee

A Modest Little Man

a play by

Francis Beckett

TSL Drama

First published in Great Britain in 2022
By TSL Publications, Rickmansworth

Copyright © 2021, 2022 Francis Beckett

ISBN / 978-1-915660-03-9

web: www.francisbeckett.co.uk

Dedication

For my late mother, Anne Cutmore,
who would have liked this play.

Characters

This play, originally called A Modest Little Man, was performed at Bread and Roses in Clapham in January 2019, then at Upstairs at the Gatehouse in Highgate in October 2019 and again in September 2021, and at the Epstein Theatre, Liverpool, in September 2022.

The cast was:

Violet Attlee	Lynne O'Sullivan
Clem Attlee	Roger Rose
Herbert Morrison	Steven Maddocks, then Pete Picton
Rose (starts as a teenage girl) / Jennie Lee	Charlotte Campbell, then Jessica Bichard, then Miranda Colmans
Winston Churchill / Hugh Dalton / John Carvel	Silas Hawkins
Vicar / King George VI / Nye Bevan	Clive Greenwood
Director	Owain Rose
Sound and lighting	Frank Turnbull

Settings

The action of the play takes place in several settings, and no attempt at realistic sets need be made. A table, three chairs and a telephone should be on the stage.

Running time

95 mins

Sound effects: shouting, cheering, celebrating, maybe a snatch of
"Land of Hope and Glory" – it's VE day, May 8 1945.
Two revellers – man in uniform, woman perhaps in nurse's uniform –
dance wildly across the stage, beer in hand, singing.

REVELLERS: Hitler has only got one ball
Goering has two, but very small
Himmler is somewhat similar
And poor old Goebbels has no balls at all.

RADIO VOICE: This is the BBC Home Service. Germany has surrendered. The war in Europe is over. The Prime Minister, Mr Churchill, will address the nation tonight. The coalition government has disbanded, and Mr Clement Attlee has relinquished his post as Deputy Prime Minister. As the leader of the Socialist Party, Mr Attlee has demanded an immediate general election.

[CHURCHILL *comes in and stands at the front, facing the audience.*]

CHURCHILL: My friends. We may allow ourselves a brief moment of rejoicing. A brief moment of dignified rejoicing.

[*The* TWO REVELLERS *dance wildly back across the stage.* CHURCHILL *is visibly annoyed at the interruption.*]

REVELLERS: [*singing to the tune of John Brown's body.*]
When the red revolution comes
When the red revolution comes
We'll made Winston Churchill scrub the steps of Number Ten
When the red revolution comes.

[CHURCHILL *looks for a moment discomposed, but recovers.*]

CHURCHILL: Yet to the east still lies the huge mass of Russia. Not a wounded Russia only, but a poisoned Russia, a plague-bearing Russia, an infected Russia. Who knows what dreadful things she might do? Russia is a riddle wrapped in a mystery inside an enigma. And there is a desperate struggle to be waged at home. For six years we have combatted Nazi tyranny abroad. We must now commence hostilities against socialist tyranny at home. The dire threat of a Socialist government is real, and we must confront it with all our might. Mr Attlee's socialists have smelled power, and will not rest until they are in control of all our destinies. My friends, I must tell you that a socialist policy is abhorrent to the British idea of freedom. No socialist government could afford to allow free, sharp or violently worded expression of public discontent. They would have to fall back on some form of Gestapo.

[*exit* CHURCHILL, *enter* VIOLET.]

VIOLET: I was so disappointed in Winston. Gestapo! To say such a thing in May 1945, with Hitler just defeated! And do you know, Clem and I had had dinner with the Churchills just the night before. The Attlees and the Churchills, just as it was during the war. Winston was charming as always. And then the very next day to say those shocking, horrible things! He seems to have forgotten rather quickly that he couldn't have won the war without Clem. Clem was loyal to Winston. Clem is a gentleman. Clem's deputy, Herbert Morrison, came to talk about how we should reply. Herbert, of course, isn't a gentleman at all.

[*exit* VIOLET.
enter ATTLEE *and* MORRISON.]

MORRISON: Clem, it's gloves off time, do you understand? That's what Winston was signalling last night. Did you see the *Daily Express*?

ATTLEE: Never read it.

MORRISON: What do you mean, you never read it? You're in politics, you're not a provincial bank manager. Look, look. "Gestapo in Britain if socialists win." What do you think of that?

ATTLEE: Suppose they've got to print something.

MORRISON: Now look, I've done this draft for your reply on the radio tonight. Are you listening? It begins: "Last night's disgraceful broadcast by the Prime Minister shows just how far into the gutter the Conservatives are prepared to sink." I think you should emphasise "gutter". Like this: "Gutter!" You'll see I've underlined it. Clem, are you listening to me?

ATTLEE: Attentively.

MORRISON: Oh, good. I'm pleased. So we're agreed then? This is what you'll say tonight? Clem, is this what you'll say tonight?

ATTLEE: Thank you, Herbert.

MORRISON: Clem, is this script all right for you?

ATTLEE: Got my own draft.

MORRISON: Oh. Perhaps you'd like to share it with me?

ATTLEE: If you wish.

[ATTLEE *takes paper from his pocket and reads.*]

ATTLEE: When I listened to the Prime Minister's broadcast last night, I realised at once what was his objective.

MORRISON: Oh dear.

ATTLEE: He wanted the electors to understand how great was the difference between Winston Churchill the great leader in war of a united nation, and Mr Churchill, the party leader of the Conservatives.

MORRISON: Listeners all over the country switch off their radios.

ATTLEE: I pay tribute to our great leader in war, the Prime Minister.

MORRISON: For heaven's sake.

ATTLEE: I understand his concern that those who accepted his leadership in war might be tempted out of gratitude to follow him further. I thank him for having disillusioned them so thoroughly.

MORRISON: That's it?

ATTLEE: Move on to other matters after that.

MORRISON: You couldn't squeeze in just one "disgraceful" could you? Or at least an "unprincipled"? I won't press you for "gutter."

ATTLEE:	Need to move on, I think.
MORRISON:	All right. All right, after this storming start, where are we going? Read on, Clem, read on.
ATTLEE:	[*reads*] The Conservative Party believes that the basis of our economic activities must be what they call private enterprise, inspired by the motive of private profit. They seem to hold that if every individual pursues his own interest, somehow or other the interest of all will be served.
MORRISON:	Well, that'll have them storming the barricades.
ATTLEE:	The country has been run on those principles for years, yet a great number of people in this country have always been badly-housed, badly-clothed, and deprived of the opportunity of work...
MORRISON:	All right, all right, that's enough. Clem, I... I sent you a letter. I wondered if you received it. Only you never replied.
ATTLEE:	Got it. Contents noted.
MORRISON:	Oh, good. You will recall, then, that I inform you of my conviction that if we are lucky enough to be elected as the government, you are not the right person to lead that government. I want you to understand that it's nothing personal. I have the highest possible personal regard for you, as you know. You do understand that, don't you?
	[ATTLEE *looks hard at* MORRISON.]
MORRISON:	People don't see you as a leader. A leader is a man with charisma. A man who can stir people. That's a leader. Someone like Winston. You're not a Winston, Clem, are you? Winston does something you don't do.
ATTLEE:	Nails his trousers to the mast. Can't get down.
MORRISON:	For heaven's sake, you know what I mean. Now, you may choose to stand down as leader. In that case, Clem, your colleagues would applaud your public

spirited sacrifice. If you don't, then after the election, the Labour MPs must be asked to elect a leader. And I shall allow my name to be put forward. As you know, I have never tried to remove you before.

[ATTLEE *grunts*.]

MORRISON: Well, all right, but there was only the once. Since you defeated me for the leadership in 1936 by a very small margin...

ATTLEE: Forty.

MORRISON: What?

ATTLEE: Forty votes. Final ballot. I got 88, you got 48.

MORRISON: Well, all right, by forty votes. Since the Party chose you as its leader, I have been loyal, I'm sure you would agree. Broadly loyal. Most of the time. Now, Clem – Clem, please listen to me. Are you listening?

ATTLEE: Attentively.

MORRISON: Clem, if by any chance we were to win the election, you will receive a summons to see the King, who will invite you to form a government.

ATTLEE: Usual procedure.

MORRISON: But Clem, you mustn't do it. It would split the Party. You must say to the King: I am sorry, Your Majesty, but I cannot agree to form a government until the Labour MPs have met and decided who they wish to lead them. You will say that, won't you, Clem?

[ATTLEE *grunts*.]

MORRISON: Well, that's a great relief. I think. And you will try to put a bit of fire into your speeches, won't you? I know it's not your style, but it's called fighting an election for a reason. You have to fight. Otherwise we'll be wiped out, and it'll be your fault.

[ATTLEE *has at last finished filling his pipe. He gets up.*]

ATTLEE: Thank you, Herbert.

[*exit* ATTLEE. MORRISON *stares after him.*]

MORRISON: [*furious*] And thank you very much.

LIGHTS DOWN.

LIGHTS UP ON VIOLET.

VIOLET: Poor, grubby little Herbert wasn't the only person who wanted Clem to lash out a bit. Nye Bevan, the great left wing hero, felt the same. Egged on, I always thought, by his dreadfully prickly wife Jennie. She was one of those women – well, if I tell you that she didn't call herself Jennie Bevan, she kept her maiden name. Jennie Lee. Very modern, I expect.

[*exit* VIOLET.
enter JENNIE *and* NYE, *talking together.*]

JENNIE: Nye, it's up to you now. Someone has to come out fighting if Attlee won't.

NYE: We can't afford to appear divided. There's an election on.

JENNIE: Churchill says these dreadful things, and Attlee – well, Attlee never says anything much, does he? He was Churchill's loyal deputy through the war. He still is, really.

NYE: No, he's our man again. I'm sure of that.

JENNIE: Our rather strange little man.

NYE: He's certainly that.

JENNIE: There's no hope of Attlee winning.

NYE: We can't change leader in the middle of an election, can we? I'm not convinced we can't win, even under Attlee.

JENNIE: Suppose we do, what then? Can you imagine a government under that little mouse doing anything? Herbert would be better. Even Herbert.

NYE: Too clever for his own good, Herbert. All ducking and diving.

JENNIE: He's his own worst enemy sometimes.

NYE:	Not while I'm alive he's not.
JENNIE:	There's a rumour that Herbert's going to try to push Attlee out after the election. He's going to challenge Attlee at the first meeting of the new MPs.
NYE:	Is he now? Where did you hear that?
JENNIE:	Where do you think?
NYE:	You hear a lot of rubbish from Hugh Dalton.
JENNIE:	He keeps his ear to the ground though.
NYE:	All right, suppose he's right. What should I do? Should I support Herbert? He's no friend of the left.
JENNIE:	At least he's something. You know he's there. He'd be a Prime Minister you didn't have to be ashamed of. If I were still in Parliament, I might support him.
NYE:	Well, I won't. You wish you were still there, don't you? Still in the thickest part of the fighting?
JENNIE:	We both wanted the same thing. We knew we were going to give our lives to it. And this is the best contribution I can make. Helping you to change the world. Because you can, Nye. I can't.
NYE:	Because it's a man's world?
JENNIE:	Partly. Men change the world. Women don't. That's how the world is. But partly because it's you, Nye. I'm married to the great Nye Bevan. I support him, as the wife of a great man should. I can't risk doing anything that might reflect badly on him. It would be an unforgiveable self-indulgence.
NYE:	You'd have left the Labour Party, Jennie, in the thirties, when everyone else did. When our comrades disappeared into the wilderness, or the Communist Party. Some of them even went to the fascists.
JENNIE:	Would I have been wrong? Now, when we might form a government, we're led by that little mouse. He'll keep you out of government, if by some miracle he wins the election.
NYE:	Then he'll have me gingering up the back benches.

JENNIE: You didn't go into politics so you could watch from the back benches while bourgeois little Clem Attlee throws away the best chance we'll ever have to make a better world.

NYE: Jennie, it's the Labour Party or nothing. I know all its faults, all its failures. But this is the Party we've taught the working class to believe in. And you know, we may be able to do something this time. Even with little Clem Attlee in charge.

JENNIE: Prove that to me, Nye. Make it worth all the years of betrayal, all the years I might have been building myself up instead of building you up.

NYE: I'll prove it. Watch me prove it.

[*they kiss.*]

JENNIE: If only Attlee had just a little bit of passion!

LIGHTS DOWN ON NYE *AND* JENNIE.

LIGHTS UP ON VIOLET, SPEAKING TO THE AUDIENCE.

VIOLET: Silly woman. If only she knew. Of course Clem had passion. He was a socialist. I didn't like it at all at first – well, I mean my parents were respectable, my brother was a clergyman, you can imagine how awkward it was, me marrying a socialist. And it's not as though he hadn't had a good education, you know, he'd been to public school. Haileybury. Field Marshals went there. But when he was a very young man, and he was going to be a barrister, back before the First World War, he went to do some good work at a sort of children's club in the East End of London. People did that in those days, do your bit for people less well off than yourself, that sort of thing. He's got a wonderful memory, he remembers to this day. He was walking past a pub in the East End one afternoon.

[*she turns to* ATTLEE *as he walks in.*]

SONG: I'm the man, the jolly fat man
That waters the workers' beer

I am the man, the very fat man
That waters the workers' beer
And what do I care if it makes them ill
If it makes them terribly queer
I've a car, a yacht, and an aeroplane,
And I waters the workers' beer.

[enter ROSE, *a teenage girl*.]

ROSE: Where are you going, Mr Attlee?

ATTLEE: I'm going home for my tea. Where are you going, Rose?

ROSE: I'm going home to see if there is any tea.

ATTLEE: Is there some doubt of that?

ROSE: Don't like to go home if I ain't earned nothing. Can't eat the food if you don't bring nothing in. Got a tanner today though.

[*she holds it out to show him*.]

ATTLEE: How did you get that?

ROSE: Poking.

ATTLEE: What?

ROSE: It's Saturday, see. Some religious folk round here, they can't poke the fire on a Saturday, it's against their religion. So when it gets cold, see, there's me just outside the door, waiting, they say, 'ere, Rosie, come an' give the fire a poke an' you'll 'ave a tanner.

ATTLEE: Very inventive. But… you've got brothers, haven't you, Rose? Don't they bring in some money?

ROSE: Four of 'em. Get to do a bit of 'umping coal some-times. Can't get regular work for love nor money. Mum and Dad and me and them in one room. Hulk-ing great brutes, they are.

ATTLEE: You can't go away to the bedroom?

ROSE: Bless you, Mr Attlee, that's the bedroom, that one room, and it's where we sit, and where we eat, and where we shit, and where my Mum and Dad they…

ATTLEE:	Yes, yes, I begin to understand.
ROSE:	Would you like me to sing you a song, Mr Attlee?
ATTLEE:	Well, now – yes, Rose, I would like that.
ROSE:	My mum sings this one all the time.
ROSE:	[*sings*] My old man said, follow the van And don't dilly dally on the way The van went ahead with me old home in it I came behind with me old cock linnet I dillied and dallied and dallied and dillied Lost me way and don't know where to roam. I dallied and dillied and dillied and dallied And I can't find my way home. [*as she sings, the* VICAR *comes in. When she sees him, she stops, embarrassed.*]
ROSE:	Sorry, Vicar.
VICAR:	Mr Attlee may be unfamiliar with that song, Rose. It's hardly edifying, I fear, Mr Attlee. It describes what's called a moonlight flit. The family are leaving in a hurry to avoid paying the rent.
ATTLEE:	Are they?
VICAR:	They are. And the line about dillying and dallying is meant to imply to the knowing audience that she dillied and dallied in public houses. She is, not to put too fine a point on it, intoxicated. Isn't that so, Rose?
ROSE:	It's just a song, Vicar. Meant no harm by it.
VICAR:	Of course not. You're a good girl, Rose. I was pleased to see you and your mother at church last Sunday. Was your father not able to come with you?
ROSE:	Wasn't well, Vicar.
VICAR:	Wasn't well, Vicar. You hear that, Mr Attlee? Wasn't well, Vicar. Is your father still drinking, Rose?
ROSE:	Don't drink no more, my dad, honest 'e don't, Vicar.
VICAR:	Is your father in work just now?
ROSE:	Looking every day, sir.

VICAR:	Well, now, Rose, I'll tell you what I'll do. You tell your mother to go round to Mrs Braithwaite's house on Wednesday, and she'll find her a day's work. How's that?
ROSE:	Clean the house out again for two bob?
VICAR:	Would your mother not want to do that?
ROSE:	Oh, no, sir, she'll do it, sir, needs the money, sir. I'd better go with her, it's a very big house.
VICAR:	Good girl. Cut along to the vestry now, my house-keeper will give you a couple of biscuits. I'd like a word with Mr Attlee.
ROSE:	Thank you kindly, Vicar.
	[*exit* ROSE.]
VICAR:	It's good to have you among us, Mr Attlee. I'd like to see more young men of good family like yourself, down here in the East End, helping those less fortu-nate than themselves.
ATTLEE:	Shouldn't be hungry. Bad show that.
VICAR:	No one need starve, Mr Attlee. In the workhouse we give them breakfast. Though I always make sure the porridge is a little burned. Don't want to give them an incentive to come to the workhouse, do we?
ATTLEE:	Shouldn't be poor.
VICAR:	On the other hand, Mr Attlee, the poor provide you with the opportunity to do good works. And good works make us blessed in the sight of the Lord. You do see that, don't you? [*he waits for a reply. Getting none, he carries on*] Well, Mr Attlee, I'm glad we were able to have this little talk. I must go and con-duct evensong. Good night to you.
	[*exit* VICAR. *Lights dimmed on* ATTLEE, *lights up on* VIOLET.]
VIOLET:	No passion! Piffle! It was Limehouse that changed his life. His mind was made up. And when his mind's made up, nothing will change it. Well, along came the Great War – you probably call it the First World

War, but back then we didn't know there was going to be another one. Clem went out to fight, and became a Major, and there he was in 1918, back in the East End after the war and wanting to stand for Parliament. For the Labour Party. Of all things! And there was dear little Rose, grown up now, she'd joined the Labour Party and knew all about speaking on street corners. And they sent her to help you. You remember it, dear?

[enter ROSE, now a young woman, singing. She is carrying a soap box.]

ROSE: If you want the Sergeant Major, we know where he is.
We know where he is.
We know where he is.
If you want the Sergeant Major, we know where he is.
He's hanging on the old barbed wire...

[she sees ATTLEE.]

ROSE: Mr Attlee! Sorry, I mean Major Attlee! I was looking for you. You won't remember me.

ATTLEE: Rose.

ROSE: It's a good few years.

ATTLEE: I have an efficient memory. I understand your poor father...

ROSE: Yes...

ATTLEE: And you had bad news from the front.

ROSE: No worse than a lot of other people. It was hard for my mother though. Still is.

ATTLEE: That song...

ROSE: My brother Harry used to sing it when he was home on leave. Right bastard, his sergeant major was, he said. Forced them over the top.

ATTLEE: Sergeant Major only doing his duty. Not an easy duty.

ROSE: You never heard the song, Major?

ATTLEE: Heard it every day. Not easy, the trenches.

ROSE: [*staring hard at* ATTLEE.] That's what I heard. Not
            fair, is it, Major Attlee?

ATTLEE: No.

ROSE: Our men do all the dying. The rich do all the living.

ATTLEE: Yes. You've changed a lot, Rose.

ROSE: I studied shorthand and typing in the evenings.
            Don't like it, but it's better than the alternative.
            We'd better get on with it. We won't get a revolu-
            tion by sitting here grumbling, will we, Major? Right,
            this is how we do it. I'll speak and you pretend to
            heckle, so they all come to see what's going on.
            That'll get an audience. Then you can get up and
            talk to them.

ATTLEE: Not sure I'm cut out for this.

ROSE: They're not educated like you. You was at Oxford,
            wasn't you?

ATTLEE: University College.

ROSE: Thought you was at Oxford?

ATTLEE: University College, Oxford.

ROSE: Oh. Right. Well, you're going to learn something
            they don't teach at University College Oxford. Don't
            forget, when I look at you, you heckle.

            [*she puts the soap box on the ground and stands on
            it and faces the audience.*]

ROSE: Comrades and friends. Go down the high street,
            what do you see? Rich folk in their cars, who made a
            killing out of the war, selling guns so poor folk could
            go out there and kill each other.

            [*she looks at* ATTLEE.]

ROSE: Major, you're supposed to heckle.

            [*turns back to audience.*]

ROSE: And then look in the gutter and you'll see the poor
            bastards who fought the war.

            [*she turns to ATTLEE expectantly.*]

ATTLEE: I disagree with your initial premise.

[ROSE *looks hard at* ATTLEE, *then decides that she will do without any help from that quarter.*]

ROSE: Some of them had their legs blown off, or their brains shot up, they're begging on the streets. And they're the lucky ones. They came back. My four brothers never come back, none of 'em, and lots of you can say something similar. And what does Lloyd George care? His friends got rich. Comrades, when Labour's in power, everything will belong to the people. So support our good friend Major Attlee here. All those bastards who did well out of the war, they better tremble, because Major Attlee's coming for them. Major Attlee.

[*clapping, she stands aside for* ATTLEE *who takes her place.*]

ATTLEE: In a civilised community, there will be some persons who will be unable at some period of their lives to look after themselves. The question of what is to happen to them may be solved in three ways. One, neglect them. Two, leave them to the goodwill of others. Three, care for them as of right by the organised community. I advocate number three.

[*he steps aside.* ROSE *realises rather late that he has finished speaking, and starts to clap enthusiastically.*]

ROSE: Comrades. Major Attlee, the leader of the socialist revolution. Three cheers for Major Attlee.

[*sings*] It's the same the 'ole world over
It's the poor what gets the blame
It's the rich what 'as the gravy
Ain't it all a bleeding shame.
Good night, Comrades. Don't forget, vote for a revolution, vote for Major Attlee.

[*she escorts* ATTLEE *out, clapping him as she goes.*]

VIOLET: Clem loved Rose. I don't mean in that way. There

was only one person Clem ever loved in that way, and that was me. But he loved her combativeness, and her fierce and unforgiving logic. When he got into Parliament he made her his secretary. That worked well until the general strike in 1926. The day after that was over, she told him she was leaving. And in the most upsetting of circumstances.

[*enter* ROSE.]

ROSE: You wanted a word, Mrs Attlee?

VIOLET: Now, Rose, the Major's quite upset. He won't say this to you himself – well, he hasn't even said it to me, you know what he's like.

ROSE: Don't say much, the Major.

VIOLET: It's not that you're leaving, though of course he'd rather you stayed. It's why you're leaving.

ROSE: It's no good, Mrs Attlee. I've made my mind up. The Labour Party betrayed the workers in the general strike. I've joined the Communist Party, and that's that.

VIOLET: What will you do for work?

ROSE: They'll give me a job on the *Daily Worker*. As a reporter. I'll be in the front line of the struggle.

VIOLET: You could work for a Labour supporting paper. The Major might be able to have a word with the editor of the *Daily Herald*.

ROSE: No, Mrs Attlee, it's not the job.

VIOLET: Perhaps you don't realise how deeply the Major feels about all these things.

ROSE: Can't imagine the Major as a revolutionary, though, can you, Mrs Attlee?

VIOLET: Well… he sings The Red Flag at the Party conference every year, you know.

ROSE: Not exactly revolutionary, is it?

VIOLET: I don't know. All that stuff about cowards flinching and traitors sneering, and their hearts' blood stain-ing its every fold, and their bones growing stiff and cold. Makes me shiver, if you want to know.

ROSE: There's a lot worse songs than that, I can tell you.

VIOLET: The Major writes poetry himself, you know.

ROSE: Does he? Doesn't seem the type somehow.

VIOLET: That day he met you outside a pub – you were a child...

ROSE: I remember it well...

VIOLET: That night he sat down and wrote a poem. I brought it to show you. Will you read it?

ROSE: You read it to me, Mrs Attlee.

VIOLET: All right. I don't often have the chance to read the Major's work aloud. It's not great poetry, mind. This is how it starts.

[*she reads.*]

VIOLET: In Limehouse, in Limehouse, today and every day
I see the weary mothers who sweat their souls away
Poor, tired mothers trying
To hush the feeble crying
Of little babies dying
For want of food today.

ROSE: The Major wrote that?

VIOLET: Yes.

ROSE: Wouldn't have thought he had it in him.

VIOLET: There's more to him than most people realise.

ROSE: I wrote a poem, too.

VIOLET: Did you, dear?

ROSE: About them bastards who sent my brothers to die. Want to hear it?

VIOLET: Yes please.

ROSE: My name is Mr Profiteer
And thoughts of taxes make me queer
Let homeless heroes starve in ditches
But don't make levies on my riches
And if the Empire needs a tax
Well, shove it on the workers' backs.
What do you think, Mrs Attlee? Not up to the

	Major's stuff, is it?
VIOLET:	It's not the Major's style exactly, Rose.
ROSE:	You can't change anything through the Labour Party. We had a Labour government, and what did it do? It didn't even try.
VIOLET:	The Major would probably agree with you.
ROSE:	But he stays in the Labour Party. The only way now is revolution, and the only Party offering that is the Communists. The Major's too staid and convention-al to do what needs to be done.
	[*exit* ROSE.]
VIOLET:	Two decades passed, neither of them any good. The poor got poorer, Ramsay Macdonald formed another Labour government which was even worse than the first one, there were hunger marches, and then there was another terrible war. Germany got Hitler and Russia got Stalin. Somewhere along the way, Clem got elected leader of the Labour Party, so he was Winston Churchill's deputy during the war. We won the war, just like we won the first one. We always seem to win wars that Clem's involved in. I expect it's just coincidence. Well, by then I'd dined with four Prime Ministers, but I never thought I might be married to one.
	[*enter* CHURCHILL.]
CHURCHILL:	It is almost inconceivable. At the end of five years and three months of world war, all our enemies having surrendered unconditionally or being about to do so, the British electorate have dismissed me from all further conduct of their affairs.
VIOLET:	I'm sure it wasn't personal, Winston. Your wife will be pleased to see more of you. Perhaps it's a bless-ing in disguise.
CHURCHILL:	It seems to be very effectively disguised.
	[*exit* CHURCHILL *and* VIOLET *as the song begins. A recording, to the tune of "John Brown's body."*]
	We'll make Winston Churchill smoke a Woodbine every day

We'll make Winston Churchill smoke a Woodbine
every day
We'll make Winston Churchill smoke a Woodbine
every day
When the red revolution comes.

[*enter* MORRISON.]

MORRISON: Clem! Clem, where are you? It's victory. We have an overall majority. And it looks like a big one. Of course it's what I expected all along. I didn't like to say anything. Clem! It would be just like him to abscond at a time like this. Clem!

[*enter* ATTLEE.]

MORRISON: Thank heavens. Now, Clem, you remember our discussion?

ATTLEE: Vividly.

MORRISON: There will soon be a summons for you to go to Buckingham Palace. I gather you have to kiss the King's hand. You must say: I cannot accept the King's commission to form a government until I have consulted my Parliamentary colleagues. Then the new Labour MPs will choose. You or me. Have you got that? Clem, I said have you got that? Have I made myself clear?

ATTLEE: Luminously.

MORRISON: Er, good. You may wish to know that my view on this has the support of several of our most senior colleagues. Some of the names would surprise you. If I told you that even Nye Bevan was considering his position. Of course they respect you, Clem, we all do, but as Prime Minister, you just won't do. If you try to form a government, you will split the Party. Don't do that, Clem. Don't go and see the King.

LIGHTS DOWN ON MORRISON *AND* ATTLEE.

Lights up on ATTLEE *and the* KING. *They stand, facing each other. Both are shy, ill at ease, neither sure what to say.*

KING: Mr Attlee.

ATTLEE:	Your Majesty.
	[*an excruciating silence.*]
ATTLEE:	I've won the election.
KING:	I know. I heard it on the six o'clock news.
	[*pause.*]
KING:	Tea?
ATTLEE:	No, thank you, Your Majesty.
KING:	No need to keep on calling me Your Majesty in the circumstances. "Sir" will be quite adequate.
ATTLEE:	Thank you, sir.
KING:	Should I send someone out with a cup of tea for your chauffeur? Must be exhausted, poor chap.
ATTLEE:	No chauffeur.
KING:	No chauffeur?
ATTLEE:	Wife drove me here.
KING:	Your wife? That's your wife waiting in the car? Mr Attlee, that's dreadful, your wife sitting out there like a servant.
ATTLEE:	She's got her boiled sweets.
KING:	We haven't even sent her out a cup of tea.
ATTLEE:	Milk. One sugar.
KING:	We can't have your wife waiting for you in your car.
	[*he picks up a telephone and speaks into it.*]
KING:	The lady in Mr Attlee's car – it's Mrs Attlee. Could you please have her brought up here to join us? Now, Mr Attlee – I'm so sorry, please sit down. Oh, I have to sit down first, don't I?
	[KING *sits.*]
KING:	Please sit down, Mr Attlee.
	[ATTLEE *sits.*]
KING:	I take it you'll form a government.
ATTLEE:	With your permission, sir.

KING:	Excellent, excellent. We – we don't actually kiss hands, you know. Sort of figure of speech, kissing hands. Embarrassing for both of us, I'm sure, kissing hands. Now, I expect you imagined Mr Churchill would win the election. Didn't you? So I don't suppose you've had much time to think about the sort of things you might want to do. [*pause*.] Mr Attlee, I said I don't suppose you've had time to think of the sort of things you want to do.
ATTLEE:	Got one or two ideas.
KING:	Yes, yes, quite. My advice, Mr Attlee, is not to try to change anything very much. Now, I know some of your wild men want you to come in and bring in some sort of workers' revolution. No good. Don't do it. Six years of war. Everyone tired. Want a quiet life.
	[ATTLEE *grunts*.]
KING:	Mr Attlee, let me be frank. The people have elected a Labour government. I don't think the country will stand for it.
ATTLEE:	Country'll get used to it.
KING:	Yes, yes, quite. But if you try to do all sorts of radical things – you do understand me, Mr Attlee?
ATTLEE:	Perfectly.
KING:	Good, good. One other thing. I understand Mr Hugh Dalton wants the Foreign Office. Don't give it to him. Dreadful gossip. Talks all the time. Great, noisy, booming voice. Old Etonian too. Makes it worse somehow.
	[ATTLEE *grunts*.]
KING:	Mr Attlee – Prime Minister – let me tell you a family secret. His father Canon Dalton was my father's tutor. My father gave his father a couple of mementoes, and this bounder gave them away. Or sold them. Give him the Exchequer, if you've got to give him something. Look after the till, about all he's fit for. That all right?
	[ATTLEE *grunts*.]

KING:	For the Foreign Office, you know, you could do worse than consider your worker chap. Trade union leader. Transport and General Workers' Union, I believe. Ernest Bevin. Talked to him once. Clever chap, considering where he came from. The English working class at its best.
	[ATTLEE *grunts*.]
KING:	Yes, well, I'm so glad we had the chance to have this little chat. Ah, here's your wife.
	[VIOLET ATTLEE *comes in. Both men stand up.*]
KING:	Mrs Attlee. A great pleasure. Won't you sit down?
	[*but she is waiting for him to sit first, and he is waiting for her.*]
VIOLET:	[*to* ATTLEE] Shouldn't he sit first?
ATTLEE:	Might as well sit down, my dear. Be here all night.
	[VIOLET *sits.* KING *sits. Last of all,* ATTLEE *sits.*]
KING:	Was the long campaign difficult for you, Mrs Attlee? I don't suppose you saw much of your husband for the last few weeks.
VIOLET:	Not at all, Your Majesty, I saw him all the time. I was his driver. I drove him everywhere during the campaign.
KING:	You… Good heavens. How very trying for you.
VIOLET:	No, no, not at all, I like it. You see, if I didn't do it, well, I don't know when we'd get to see each other, and anyway he doesn't want some stranger driving him, does he, not with all the things he's got on his mind. It's something I can do for him, you see.
KING:	You must have driven hundreds of miles.
ATTLEE:	3,597.
KING:	How on earth do you know that?
VIOLET:	He loves exact things like that, Clem. He loves knowing exactly what number of miles I've driven, and

	exactly how many I'm going to drive tomorrow, and the names of everyone in his class at school.
KING:	Everyone in his class at school? He's 61 years old.
VIOLET	I came home one night during the war and he'd just written out the names of every boy in his class at Haileybury School when he was 13. Can you believe that?
KING:	Remarkable.
VIOLET:	Anyway, if I didn't drive him, who would iron his trousers?
KING:	Iron his trousers?
VIOLET:	I carry a portable iron, you see, these days you can't rely on hotels to have that sort of thing, not with the rationing and everything, so I carry... Not that it always works.
KING:	The iron doesn't always work?
VIOLET:	No, the iron always works, but Clem, you see, he insists on carrying his pipe and tobacco pouch in his pocket...
KING:	In his trouser pocket?
VIOLET:	No, in his jacket pocket, you see, and the thing is, it doesn't give a suit any chance, pulls it right out of shape. I've said it to him over and over.
KING:	I'm sure you have.
VIOLET:	But it doesn't do any good. Well, he has a lot on his mind, I expect he forgets. He always grunts when I tell him.
KING:	He grunts?
VIOLET:	Yes, grunts. But it never makes any difference.
KING:	How very upsetting.
VIOLET:	Not really. Not to me, anyway. I like to hear him grunt. That way I know he's there.
KING:	Well, at least during the next election we can relieve you of your chauffeuring duties, Mrs Attlee. I'm sure a government car and chauffeur would be available for the Prime Minister.

VIOLET:	Oh, no, you mustn't do that, we like it as we are, we have those long days together. When I don't know the way he has the atlas on his knee. When I know where I'm going he does the *Times* crossword. Every so often he puts a boiled sweet in my mouth.
KING:	A very affecting scene. All the same... Mr Attlee, you must help me persuade you wife – these long jour-neys must be a strain on her.
ATTLEE:	Prefer to keep things as they are.
KING:	No, I insist. Mr Attlee, you must allow me to insist.
ATTLEE:	Rather have my wife driving me, thank you, sir.
KING:	Well. Very well. Now, I am sure the new Prime Minister has many matters to attend to...
	[VIOLET *gets up.*]
VIOLET:	Yes, yes, come on Clem, we can't keep His Majesty all night, anyway I don't want the car to cool down too much, sometimes you know it takes ages to start, you remember that time in somewhere north-ern, St Albans I think it was, we had to get Mr Phil-pott from the *Daily Herald* to crank the engine. He was covering the election and we gave him a lift, and when the car wouldn't go, well, I wouldn't have troubled Mr Philpott, but you see Clem had his clean suit on.
KING:	Goodnight, Mrs Attlee.
VIOLET:	Good night, Your Majesty.
	[*she curtsies.*]
KING:	Mr Attlee.
ATTLEE:	Good night, sir.
VIOLET:	Come along, Clem.
	[*the ATTLEES go out. As they leave,* VIOLET *takes CLEM's hand.*]
KING:	Clem, eh? Clam would be more appropriate.
	[*exit KING. Singing on sound effects, again to the tune of John Brown's body.*]

We'll turn Buckingham Palace into a block of council flats
We'll turn Buckingham Palace into a block of council flats
We'll turn Buckingham Palace into a block of council flats
When the red revolution comes.

[enter, from opposite sides, MORRISON and HUGH DALTON.]

MORRISON: Hugh. Have you seen Attlee? He's disappeared.

DALTON: Well, he's barely visible at the best of times. A modest little man, our Clem.

MORRISON: With plenty to be modest about. So where is he?

DALTON: I believe he's with the King.

MORRISON: With the King?

DALTON: I'm afraid so.

MORRISON: He shouldn't have done that, Hugh. This will cause a lot of trouble in the Party. I told him. I said, the new intake must have their say. They're not going to have an insignificant little man like Clem Attlee leading them at this great moment in history.

DALTON: And you would have had my support, Herbert. I told you that. I was with you all the way.

MORRISON: There'll be a vote of no confidence at the first meeting of the Parliamentary Labour Party. You can propose it.

DALTON: Herbert, you know I'd do anything...

MORRISON In my government you'd be Foreign Secretary.

DALTON: In Attlee's too, I've no doubt. It could be the little man's dished you, Herbert.

MORRISON: We'll see about that. It's not over yet.

[enter ATTLEE. He goes to his desk.]

MORRISON: You had no right to go to the King.

ATTLEE:	[*without looking up.*] Usual practice.
MORRISON:	If you don't open up the issue of the leadership, we will. Isn't that right, Hugh?
DALTON:	Well, I certainly think it would be wise to open it up. Prudent. More than prudent. Judicious. Definitely.
MORRISON:	If you don't open up the leadership, where does that leave me?
ATTLEE:	Deputy PM.
MORRISON:	Is that all?
ATTLEE:	Thought you could run the nationalisation programme.
MORRISON:	I meant what I said. I intend to take the leadership issue to the first meeting of the new Labour MPs. Hugh will support me. Won't you, Hugh?
DALTON:	Well...
MORRISON:	There'll be a lot of support, you can rely on that.
DALTON:	Wouldn't do it, Herbert. Too late. Take the offer, that's my advice. It's not a bad offer. Big stuff, nationalisation.
MORRISON:	What, working on economic stuff with bloody Ernest Bevin at the Exchequer, looking over my shoulder all the time and telling me what to do.
ATTLEE:	Bevin's not going to be Chancellor.
DALTON:	He's not? What are you going to do with him then?
ATTLEE:	Foreign Secretary.
DALTON:	Clem, are you mad? Ernie Bevin going off to talk to foreign governments. Ernie Bevin talking to sophisticated French bureaucrats, the cream of the *grandes ecoles*. Ernie Bevin having a cosy chat with the smart Harvard men at the State Department.
ATTLEE:	Doesn't have your advantages.
DALTON:	Of course, of course, I don't mean to... does well for a man without education, one has to respect that, naturally, but Clem, what does he know? He probably

	thinks the Soviet Union is a breakaway from the Transport and General Workers' Union. Clem, I was to have the Foreign Office. What's to become of me?
ATTLEE:	Trained economist. You'll be Chancellor.
DALTON:	Ernie Bevin, Foreign Secretary! It doesn't bear thinking about. Do you know, I stood him lunch the other day at the Savoy. Thought I ought to introduce him to London's finer places to eat. Turns out he goes there every day. Know what he says to the head waiter? "Bottle o'newts, Gaston. Bottle o'newts." Head waiter didn't turn a hair.
MORRISON:	Bottle of newts? What on earth did he want a bottle of newts for?
DALTON:	Two minutes later the head waiter was back carrying a bottle of Nuits St Georges. He calls it newts. Apparently he asks for one every day. Gaston has learned to translate raw Bevin into English.
ATTLEE:	Perhaps other nations' foreign ministers will prove as perceptive as the head waiter at the Savoy.
MORRISON:	Shame, really, you not going to the Foreign Office, Hugh. That would have put an end to secret diplomacy.
DALTON:	Any other cabinet surprises you'd like to share with us, Prime Minister?
ATTLEE:	Bringing Nye Bevan into cabinet.
DALTON:	You're what?
MORRISON:	It's less than a year since we had to expel him from the Party.
DALTON:	He's completely undisciplined.
MORRISON:	He doesn't know the meaning of loyalty.
DALTON:	What are you thinking of giving him?
ATTLEE:	Health and Housing.
MORRISON:	Those are the two biggest portfolios in government. If we fail on those, we fail on everything.
DALTON:	I beg you, think about it.

ATTLEE:	Appointed him this morning.
DALTON:	So I'm to go to the Exchequer and find the money for Nye Bevan to spend. Well, we'd better hope our American friends don't stop lend-lease.
MORRISON:	Do we still need lend-lease, Hugh, now the war's over?
DALTON:	Need it? If we can't get food and materials from the USA on tick, we're finished.
MORRISON:	Bad as that?
DALTON:	Clem, as your new Chancellor perhaps I should make the facts clear to you. If the Americans cut off lend-lease now – if, suddenly, we have to pay on the nail for everything we import from them – this country will starve. And I mean starve. Within weeks.
MORRISON:	And you've just appointed Nye Bevan to start some sort of nationalised health service. How do you think that's going to go down in Washington?
DALTON:	I can hear some of the Neanderthals in Congress now. [*puts on American accent*] Those limeys running socialised medicine on our money for chrissake.
MORRISON:	You can't do it, Clem. You can't let Nye ruin us all.
DALTON:	There will be a row in the Party about it.
MORRISON:	As you know, Clem, I'm loyal to a fault, but I may not feel able in all conscience to defend you this time. Clem, are you listening? Have you heard a word of what we've been saying?
ATTLEE:	Clear as a bell.

LIGHTS DOWN.

LIGHTS UP ON NYE BEVAN *AND* JENNIE LEE.

JENNIE:	Housing and Health! He's given you a real job! Did you take it?
NYE:	Took it! I practically bit his hand off.

JENNIE:	I thought he'd try and fob you off with some trinket. Under Secretary at the Ministry of paperclips. What did he say?
NYE:	I can remember every word. [*imitates* ATTLEE's *voice*] I understand you have much experience of negotiation. I am offering you a post where you will deal with health, housing and the local authorities.
JENNIE:	Just like him. No passion. What did you say?
NYE:	He obviously wanted me to leave. I'd taken up a full 45 seconds of his time already.
JENNIE:	Why on earth has he done it?
NYE:	I can't imagine. But I don't care. Jennie, everything I've ever done has been a preparation for this. When I'm done, no one will ever suffer pain or die of a treatable illness because they haven't got the money to pay for the treatment. My father, lying there choking on the coal dust...
JENNIE:	Has it occurred to you that Attlee's setting you up to fail?
NYE:	What do you mean?
JENNIE:	He's given you the toughest job in government. If he doesn't give you his backing every inch of the way, they'll tear you to pieces – the press, the doctors. And he can say, well, I tried to make a better world, but Nye Bevan wasn't up to it, sorry everyone.
NYE:	I won't fail. Jenny, I won't fail.
	[*enter* HUGH DALTON.]
DALTON:	Nye. I understand congratulations are in order.
JENNIE:	Why did Attlee do it? Do you know, Hugh? He's such a cautious, bourgeois little man. Politics to him isn't a fierce struggle for a better world. It's a lazy afternoon at one of his beloved cricket matches.
DALTON:	Between ourselves, Jennie, I suggested this appointment to the PM. Bring in Nye, I said, he'll be loyal if you give him a real job of work to do.
NYE:	Thank you, Hugh.

DALTON:	Not at all. My pleasure.
NYE:	You're to be Chancellor, I hear. Hope you're not too disappointed.
DALTON:	Not at all. It's what I wanted. I trained in economics, you know.
JENNIE:	I heard you were after the Foreign Office.
DALTON:	What, me? Me having to deal with slimy French bureaucrats, the cream of the so-called *grandes ecoles*? Me sucking up to preppy young Harvard men at the State Department? No thank you. I said to the PM, I want a job with real power, give me the Exchequer.
NYE:	It means you'll have to find the money for my National Health Service.
DALTON:	Well, there's a bit of an obstacle now, of course.
JENNIE:	Why? What's happened?
DALTON:	Haven't you... no, no, of course, it's – I shouldn't have said anything. My apologies.
NYE:	What's going on, Hugh?
DALTON:	I shouldn't have said anything. Only for the top three in government. Please forgive me.
NYE:	Remember I'm in the cabinet now.
DALTON:	Well, yes, but...
	[*he looks meaningfully at* JENNIE.]
NYE:	You don't want to say it in front of Jennie? You know us, Hugh. You know I'll tell her anyway.
JENNIE:	Come on, Hugh, out with it. You know you're going to in the end. You can't help yourself.
DALTON:	Well, strictly between ourselves.
	[*he gathers them, one each side of him, pulls them close and speaks confidentially.*]
DALTON:	There's a bit of a problem with our friends on the other side of the Atlantic.
NYE:	You don't mean...

[JENNIE *puts her fingers to her lips and* NYE *stops.*]

DALTON: If only Roosevelt had lived. Roosevelt understood the situation. I explained it to him myself. We're old friends, you know, Franklin and I. "This is how it is, Franklin," I said. He was grateful. "Thank you, Hugh," he said. Franklin dying last month was a disaster. Harry Truman isn't ready to be president. Dear Harry. A good chap, but hopelessly provincial.

NYE: But what's he done, Hugh? What's he done?

DALTON: What's he done? He's gone and cancelled lend-lease, that's what he's done.

NYE: That's torn it.

JENNIE: The little man will cave in now, won't he? Nye, you need to get to Clem before he panics.

NYE: He'll give in. He's bound to. Poor little chap, he won't see there's another way.

JENNIE: Tell him, just because there's a crisis, it doesn't mean the people don't need homes.

NYE: I'll try to see him now.

[*exit* NYE.]

JENNIE: Truman will give us a little time, won't he? A few weeks to build up stocks of food.

DALTON: None. Nothing.

JENNIE: Nothing?

DALTON: Not a second. There's a ship in the middle of the Atlantic, loaded to the gunnels with food for Britain, and it's been ordered to turn round and sail straight back to New York. The only hope is an American loan. Jennie, you'll have to tell Nye – this makes a real mess of our plans. Welfare state. Nationalisation. The Americans won't like any of that. We'll have to trim all that back. We've got to have the money.

JENNIE: I'm not telling Nye that.

DALTON: You're the only one he'll listen to.

JENNIE:	That's exactly why I'm not telling him.
DALTON:	Oh God. Then we're back to whatever little Clem Attlee can pull off in Washington.
JENNIE:	Clem's going to Washington?
DALTON:	Addressing both houses of Congress, no less. Little Clem Attlee! Speaking to Congress! He's the worst speaker in the world.

LIGHTS DOWN

LIGHTS UP ON VIOLET.

VIOLET:	And slippery, snobbish Hugh Dalton thought my Clem wasn't good enough to address the US Congress. We showed them, didn't we, Clem? We did it.
	[*exit* VIOLET. ATTLEE *comes to the front and speaks from a lectern.*]
ATTLEE:	There is, and always will be, scope for enterprise, but when big business gets too powerful, so that it becomes monopolistic, we hold it is not safe to leave it in private hands. Further, in the world today, we believe that we must plan the economic activities of our country if we are to assure the common man a fair deal.

LIGHTS DOWN ON ATTLEE.

LIGHTS UP ON ATTLEE, DALTON, NYE, MORRISON, *ALL READING A PAPER.* DALTON *PUTS IT DOWN AND BREAKS THE SILENCE.*

DALTON:	Well, it'll do. It's not what we hoped. Less money, more interest, and we have to agree to all sorts of nasty things. Ernie says the American Secretary of State has just been on the phone to tell him all the places we own where they'd like to have bases for their military. Apparently he made it pretty clear that if he didn't get them, the loan was off.
MORRISON:	I rather expected they might demand we restructure our government.
NYE:	You mean fire me?

MORRISON:	A restructure might involve that.
DALTON:	I understand the PM told the President he wasn't prepared to discuss that.
MORRISON:	Really?
ATTLEE:	Matter for the British government.
MORRISON:	We might have got a better deal if you hadn't stood on your dignity.
DALTON:	I was rather hoping they might relax on sharing their nuclear secrets. We gave them our nuclear research during the war, after all.
MORRISON:	We'll just have to start from scratch.
DALTON:	The cost is extortionate.
MORRISON:	No choice. The Russians are close to getting one.
NYE:	So the Russians have got one, so we have to have one, so they have to have a bigger one. Where does it end?
MORRISON:	We have to be able to defend ourselves. Winston was right about the Russians. They've pushed east as far as Poland. They have to be stopped somewhere.
NYE:	It'll have to come out of the defence budget then.
MORRISON:	Not a chance. The PM's already promised the Americans we'll set an example to Europe. He sets a lot of store by this North Atlantic treaty.
NYE:	So we're going to spend all our money on killing people instead of curing them! Not if there's anything I can do to stop it. We're spending that money on a national health service.
MORRISON:	No national health service now, I'm afraid.
NYE:	Herbert, the whole point of having a Labour government…
MORRISON:	It's not just your department that'll suffer, Nye. My nationalisation proposals. Unemployment pay…
NYE:	You're going to leave folk to starve, just as though the thirties were still with us?
DALTON:	Education…
NYE:	Christ, we're socialists. You got to teach everyone to read and write.

MORRISON:	Of course you have, in the long run, but we can't afford it now.
NYE:	I don't see how I can stay in the government if…
MORRISON:	Are you threatening to resign?
DALTON:	I wouldn't answer that if I were you, Nye.
NYE:	We were elected to make the lives of the poor tolerable. We've got to get on with it. And you know what, if Uncle Sam doesn't like it he can stick his…
ATTLEE:	Thank you all.
DALTON:	That it then, Clem?
NYE:	I just want to clear up this question of the atom bomb.
MORRISON:	PM says meeting's over.
	[*all rise and start to go except* ATTLEE.]
ATTLEE:	Nye. Could you stay behind a moment? Like a word.
	[NYE *sits down again; exit* MORRISON *and* DALTON.]
NYE:	Clem, I hope you realise – I'm not seeking confrontation, but I have to fight my corner. Clem, the National Health Service is what this government's about. Look, I know Ernie's obsessed by this bomb. He's got Russian communists on the brain, Ernie.
	[ATTLEE *grunts.*]
NYE:	Clem, I know it must be a temptation to let Ernie have his atom bomb and buy peace in the Party, and I don't want to appear to blackmail you, but you know, I'd be under a lot of pressure to resign and to…. Clem, are you listening?
ATTLEE:	Didn't wear your dinner jacket at the Mansion House.
NYE:	What?
ATTLEE:	Dinner jacket. Usual dress at Mansion House dinner.
NYE:	Oh, God. I suppose bloody Herbert showed you the press stories. Nye Bevan didn't wear a dinner jacket to the Mansion House dinner, shock horror. Clem, I don't own a dinner jacket. Jennie would never stand

	for it. Uniform of the ruling classes, she says.
ATTLEE:	Think you should buy one.
NYE:	But why? How can I be a better health and housing minister because I own a dinner jacket?
ATTLEE:	Not the battle we're here to fight. Distraction.
NYE:	Well, Clem, if you insist, but can I just make the point that...
ATTLEE:	Good chap. See you at cabinet.
NYE:	Well, I'll – I'll be off then?

[*but* ATTLEE *is already back at work.* NYE *goes out;*
enter DALTON.]

DALTON:	Clem, I wonder if I might have a word.
ATTLEE:	Yes, Hugh?
DALTON:	It's the defence estimates. They're a lot higher than I'd expected. You see, Clem, it throws everything out. More borrowing. More debt. What's it all for?
ATTLEE:	Need to be able to defend ourselves.
DALTON:	How's it to be allocated?
ATTLEE:	Special mechanism.
DALTON:	Special cabinet committee?
ATTLEE:	Yes.
DALTON:	Clem. I see you've set up a small administrative committee, which I'm not on. Gen 75. Has that got something to do with defence?
ATTLEE:	Yes.
DALTON:	Do I need to know what it's for?
ATTLEE:	No.
DALTON:	Clem, as you know I'm the last man to stand on his dignity.
ATTLEE:	Yes.
DALTON:	How are you going to break it to Nye that his dreams are over? He still thinks he's going to have his

	National Health Service and millions of new council houses - and along the way you'll throw in enough money to raise the school leaving age, hand out unemployment pay... Clem, you've made Nye the darling of the left. If he resigns now he'll split the Party. Do you want me to handle it?
ATTLEE:	Handle what?
DALTON:	Telling Nye it's over, we can't have both a welfare state and huge defence spending.
ATTLEE:	We can.
DALTON:	The tax rises you'd need would be....
ATTLEE:	Yes.
DALTON:	Oh dear.
	[*pause*.]
DALTON:	Clem, we've known each other a long time. Can I speak frankly?
ATTLEE:	Yes.
DALTON:	Look, the thing is, Herbert's been plotting. I expect you know that.
ATTLEE:	Yes.
DALTON:	Yes. Well, the long and the short of it is, he's been saying, ecomomic crisis, we need a PM who can rally the people, a PM who can explain to our people why they can't have all the good things they want, we should get Clem to resign and get Ernie Bevin to take over. I have to say, Clem, I think he has a point.
ATTLEE:	Ernie?
DALTON:	Yes.
	[ATTLEE *picks up telephone*.]
ATTLEE:	Ernie? Clem. I've got Hugh here. He says you want my job. I see. I see. I see. Thought so. [*puts phone down*.] Ernie isn't interested. Cabinet tomorrow. Don't be late.

LIGHTS DOWN ON ATTLEE *AND* DALTON.

LIGHTS UP ON NYE *AND* JENNIE.

JENNIE:	You agreed? You said you'd buy a dinner jacket?
NYE:	You think I should resign over a dinner jacket?
JENNIE:	He probably thinks I put you up to it.
NYE:	He probably does. He thinks you're a bad influence. He told Dalton so.
JENNIE:	He told Dalton? But he knows Dalton can't keep his mouth shut. Dalton was bound to tell you.
NYE:	Probably intended that.
JENNIE:	What did he say to Dalton?
NYE:	[*imitates* ATTLEE's *voice.*] Nye needed a sedative. He got an irritant.
JENNIE:	Horrid, prissy, bourgeois little man! And this is our Labour Prime Minister! This is the man who's going to make a revolution!
NYE:	Aren't you forgetting something?
JENNIE:	Yes, Nye. I'm forgetting you. As long as you're in government, there's hope.

[*he starts to sing quietly, and she joins in.*]

We'll make Clement Attlee scrub the steps of Transport House
We'll make Clement Attlee scrub the steps of Transport House
We'll make Clement Attlee scrub the steps of Transport House
When the red revolution comes.

NYE:	Believe in me, Jennie. I can't do it unless you believe in me.

[NYE *kisses her and goes out.* JENNIE *watches him. Enter from other side of stage,* VIOLET. JENNIE *does not see her until she speaks.*]

VIOLET:	You must be very proud of him, Jennie.
JENNIE:	Violet. Vi. I didn't see you. Yes. Yes, I suppose I am.
VIOLET:	And you feel you're making a contribution, don't you? As he goes out and changes the world, you

	know he couldn't do it without you. I feel that about Clem.
JENNIE:	I'm sure you do.
VIOLET:	Always a clean shirt. Always a kind word. That's it, isn't it?
JENNIE:	Not quite, no.
VIOLET:	Behind every great man...
JENNIE:	It's not quite the same for me. We've got a shared vision, Nye and I. Whereas you and Clem – I mean – well, politics isn't really your subject, is it, Vi?

[VIOLET *freezes a little*.]

VIOLET:	I expect you think I'm a little mouse. Always running around after Clem, doing silly domestic things.
JENNIE:	No, no...
VIOLET:	A doormat. A musical doormat, waiting to play "See the conquering hero comes" when her husband walks on it.
JENNIE:	Not at all.
VIOLET:	I can't wait to see the great Nye Bevan in his dinner jacket.
JENNIE:	What!
VIOLET:	Uniform of the ruling classes, he used to call it.
JENNIE:	Your husband told you about the dinner jacket!
VIOLET:	He tells me gossipy things like that. He thinks they'll amuse me. And sometimes, they do.
JENNIE:	You don't talk about real politics then?
VIOLET:	My dear, when you've been dealing with affairs of state all day, the last thing you want to come home to is a wife who wants to talk about the national health service.
JENNIE:	That's not true of Nye.
VIOLET:	Isn't it, dear? Perhaps you're right. I must be off. Clem's due in the flat in half an hour. Need to have tea ready.

[*exit* VIOLET.]

JENNIE:	You'll never wear that bloody dinner jacket, Nye. Not while I'm alive.
	[*exit* JENNIE. *Enter* MORRISON *reading a newspaper and carrying a pile of them under his arm.*]
NYE:	Not pretty reading this morning, our press lords' newspapers, are they, Herbert?
MORRISON:	They've thrown everything they've got at you. At us, I suppose I should say.
NYE:	You bet they bloody have.
MORRISON:	Nye, I know you enjoy winding the press up, but I fear for the survival of the government if this goes on.
NYE:	You want to stop reading the papers, Herbert. They're bad for your blood pressure.
MORRISON:	They've all led on that speech by the chairman of the British Medical Association.
NYE:	The bastard who says I'm Hitler.
MORRISON:	People believe it. That's the trouble.
NYE:	No one believes it, Herbert, the man's a lying scoundrel. Have you seen his speech? I mean the real speech, not what the press made of it. I've got it here. Listen. [*reads*] "The so-called National Health Service is the first step towards National Socialism as practised in Germany. The bill could be written in two lines: I take power to dictate exactly what medical treatment everyone gets, signed Aneurin Bevan, fuhrer."
MORRISON:	It's deadly, that.
NYE:	But why should anyone believe it?
MORRISON:	We spent six years fighting Hitler.
NYE:	But it's a lie.
MORRISON:	It's a lie that lodges in people's brains. Once it's there, you can't dig it out again.
NYE:	Listen, listen. [*reads*] "It is part of a socialist plot to convert Great Britain into a National Socialist

economy. The doctors will not work in Bevan's concentration camp, and there is nothing that Bevan or any other socialist can do about it in the shape of Hitler-like coercion." [*stops reading*] I mean, Herbert, it's just saying a lie over and over.

MORRISON: The more often you say a lie, the more people believe it. That's what the Nazis understood. It's what Goebbels taught us.

NYE: So we're learning from the bloody Nazis now, are we?

MORRISON: I tell you, Nye, when Fascism comes here, it won't be called fascism, it'll be called making Britain great again.

NYE: And it'll be led by those newspapers you're so fond of.

MORRISON: Beaverbrook's newspapers, Rothermere's newspapers, they pick up the lie and run with it. [*picks of newspapers one by one*] "Heil Bevan. We won't work in Bevan's Nazi system say doctors. The Health Minister, Mr Aneurin Bevan, is poised to turn Britain's hospitals into concentration camps."

NYE: We can't set policy on the basis of lies.

MORRISON: Lies that people believe. Here's another. "Mr Bevan demands the power to decide who lives and who dies. We say to *Obergruppenfuher* Aneurin Bevan what we said to Adolf Hitler."

NYE: I have to hit back hard. I've drafted a speech...

MORRISON: You'd better get the PM's permission to deliver it. Or you'll be out on your ear.

NYE: He's looking at it now.

MORRISON: Mind if I take a look.

[NYE *hands it over.*]

MORRISON: [*reading*] Tories are lower than vermin blah blah... Lord Rothermere, owner of the *Daily Mail*, was

Hitler's cheerleader in Britain blah blah... Grovelling journalists creeping round this disgusting Nazi press lord blah blah... doctors' leaders are child murderers... [*he throws the speech on the table*] For heaven's sake, Nye. You're a cabinet minister. You can't talk like that.

NYE: Just bloody watch me.

[*enter* ATTLEE, *with* NYE's *speech in his hands. The other two watch him. Pause.*]

NYE: Have you had a chance to look over my speech yet, Clem?

MORRISON: We can't afford the confrontation.

NYE: We can't afford not to hit back.

MORRISON: I tell you what we can't afford, Nye, we can't afford your National Health Service. We haven't the money, and we haven't the political capital.

NYE: Then what the hell are we in government for?

MORRISON: Your scheme's identified with the Nazis now, in everyone's mind. Clem, we have to stop Nye making that speech. And we have to look again at this National Health Service. It could endanger the government. Clem, I beg you... Have you been listening at all, Clem?

ATTLEE: Speech isn't any good, Nye. Don't make it.

MORRISON: That's right, that's right. Clem, we need to talk about the opposition to Nye's plan.

NYE: Clem.

ATTLEE: If you're going to negotiate with a man tomorrow, don't insult him today.

NYE: Negotiate? What the hell am I supposed to negotiate?

ATTLEE: See what doctors want. They probably want money.

[*exit* ATTLEE.]

MORRISON: What the hell does he mean by that?

NYE: I'm not sure, Herbert. But I'm thinking about it.

LIGHTS DOWN ON NYE AND MORRISON.

LIGHTS UP. ATTLEE *working on papers.*

Enter DALTON.

DALTON: You wanted to see me, Clem?

ATTLEE: Press got your budget speech while you were still on your feet. Bad show that.

DALTON: Oh, Clem! All I said to Carvel of the Star was "penny on fags, tuppence on a pint." That's all he had.

ATTLEE: Have to go.

DALTON: [*Looking round him.*] Go where?

ATTLEE: Have to resign.

DALTON: But Clem - there was no dishonesty, I'm not on the take, no harm was done, no run on the pound, nothing like that.

ATTLEE: Undermines faith in government all the same. Government has to be seen to be completely clean.

[ATTLEE *returns to his papers.*]

DALTON: Clem.

[*No response.* DALTON *leaves, crushed.*]

[VIOLET *comes in behind Attlee and put her hands on his shoulders. He looks up, smiles and carries on. She rubs his shoulders. Eventually she speaks.*]

VIOLET: When I got up this morning, I found all my wool tidied up round my needles. I left it in the most terrible mess. I don't know how you do it.

ATTLEE: [*still working.*] Nice to have a problem with a solution.

VIOLET: Will you finish early enough to read me another chapter of *Pride and Prejudice* tonight? We'd got to...

ATTLEE: Darcy about to declare love for Elizabeth Bennett.

VIOLET: You always remember. What's that?

[*she picks a piece of paper from the heap in front of him and reads.*] Would you please explain, dear

Clement
Just why it has to be
That Certificates of Education
Are barred to such as me?

ATTLEE: Teenage girl sent it in apparently. Sent to education department. Came to me because Tomlinson's ill, I suppose.

VIOLET: Is that your reply?
[*she reads.*] I received with real pleasure
Your verses, my dear Ann.
Although I've not much leisure
I'll reply as best I can.
I've not the least idea why
They have this curious rule
Condemning you to sit and sigh
Another year at school.
You'll understand that my excuse
For lack of detailed knowledge
Is that school certs were not in use
When I attended college.
George Tomlinson is ill, but I
Will ask him to explain
And when I know the reason why
I'll write to you again.
Clem, it's lovely.

ATTLEE: Best not send it though.

[*he takes it back and puts it at the bottom of his papers. Enter MORRISON.*]

MORRISON: Clem, there are two journalists waiting for you. Your press office said you'd see them.

ATTLEE Francis Williams said that?
VIOLET: I'm sorry, I was meant to tell you. It's Mr Carvel from *The Star* and a young lady from the *Daily Herald* – I didn't catch her name.

MORRISON: You have to give them ten minutes each.

VIOLET: Does he have to, Herbert? He's been working non-stop for 14 hours.

MORRISON: Yes, he has to. And see Carvel first, *The Star*

matters. Talk to the *Daily Herald*, you're only talking to people who are going to vote Labour anyway, so they don't matter. And Carvel's a chum of Hugh Dalton's. Dalton talks to him a lot.

ATTLEE: Dalton talks to a journalist?

MORRISON: Of course.

ATTLEE: Why would he want to do that?

MORRISON: I'm not sure where to start. Clem, you do know, don't you, that Carvel was the journalist Dalton leaked his budget to.

ATTLEE: I see.

MORRISON: He used to be on our side, as far as his paper let him. He thinks you were too hard on Hugh. We'd like him back on side. Look, just see Carvel first, will you?

VIOLET: I'll keep the lady from the *Herald* company. Come on, Herbert.

[*exit* VIOLET *and* MORRISON. ATTLEE *carries on working. Enter* CARVEL.]

CARVEL: Prime Minister, so grateful you could spare the time. Shall we start? Prime Minister, I said shall we start?

ATTLEE: Yes.

CARVEL: Well, now, Prime Minister, thank you for seeing me. I imagine you find your new responsibilities quite daunting. The atomic bomb, a world with the capacity to destroy itself, such diverse personalities as President Truman and Marshal Stalin. I am sure you feel the weight of your new responsibilities.

ATTLEE: Yes.

CARVEL: Yes, I thought you'd feel that. Mm. Of course your wartime experience as deputy to Mr Churchill will have helped, in enabling you to comprehend what is required of you. I'm sure that experience is a help to you. Prime Minister, is your wartime experience as deputy to Mr Churchill a help to you in coping with your present responsibilities?

ATTLEE: Yes.

CARVEL:	Yes, I thought you'd feel that too. Well. Prime Minister. Your colleague Mr Bevan's proposed National Health Service has come in for criticism. It has been compared to systems in countries which have, shall we say, a view of freedom which is at variance with ours in Britain. I wonder whether you feel, Prime Minister, that there is reason to consider the proposals undemocratic, inimical to freedom, and frankly un-British?
ATTLEE:	No.
CARVEL:	You don't feel you are perhaps denying the individual the freedom to take their own decisions?
ATTLEE:	Not in the slightest.
	[CARVEL *waits for him to continue, but he does not continue.*]
CARVEL:	No. Well. Turning now to your colleague Mr Jim Griffiths' proposals for unemployment pay, the scheme is surely wide open to abuse. How can you ensure that it will never be abused?
ATTLEE:	Better have it abused than let people starve.
CARVEL:	Surely the prevention of starvation ought to be the business of charitable people, churches, charities, rather than the business of the state?
ATTLEE:	Nonsense.
CARVEL:	Would you like to elaborate on that a little?
ATTLEE:	Utter nonsense.
CARVEL:	Yes. Well, Prime Minister, the religious community takes a very different view, as I'm sure you know. In fact, the leader of Britain's Catholics, Cardinal Griffin, has said: "It will be a sad day for England when charity becomes an affair of the state." What do you have to say to Cardinal Griffin?
ATTLEE:	Charity never stopped starvation. Only the state does that.
CARVEL:	So you reject the unanimous view of all parts of Britain's Christian community? You seem to have a

	low opinion of the Christian religion and its leaders. What do you think of Christianity, if I may ask that?
ATTLEE:	Agree with the ethics. Can't abide the mumbo jumbo.
CARVEL:	May I press you a little further on your attitude to religion...
ATTLEE:	No.
CARVEL:	With respect, Prime Minister, I think there's a legitimate public interest in your religious views.
	[*he waits.* ATTLEE *says nothing.* CARVEL *blinks first.*]
CARVEL:	Well. Turning now to Mr Herbert Morrison's proposals to nationalise the railways, and Mr Shinwell's proposals to nationalise the mines. In what way do you think the state is qualified to run these great industries?
ATTLEE:	Private owners made a mess of them.
CARVEL:	Would you like to elaborate on that?
ATTLEE:	No.
CARVEL:	Well. Your Education Minister's proposals will have the effect of ensuring that every child up to the age of 15 goes to school. Now, it has been argued that the education of our children is no business of the state. The churches have fulfilled this responsibility for many years, and it should not be taken away from them by the state. How do you justify spending very substantial sums in tax revenue on education?
ATTLEE:	Everyone should be taught to read and write.
CARVEL:	Turning to foreign affairs, Prime Minister, many members of your Party are concerned at rising defence expenditure and your committment to the North Atlantic Treaty Organisation.
ATTLEE:	Thought your paper was in favour of that?
CARVEL:	We are, but aren't you going to have internal troubles with the Labour Party?
ATTLEE:	Expect so.

CARVEL:	Off the record, Prime Minister, is there any chance of bringing Hugh Dalton back into the cabinet? It was an innocent mistake, and my fault for pressing him.
ATTLEE:	No. That it then?
CARVEL:	Is there anything else you'd like to say to the readers of *The Star*, Prime Minister?
ATTLEE:	Don't think so, no. Got everything you want?
CARVEL	Well, in a manner of speaking, Prime Minister.
ATTLEE:	Goodbye then.
CARVEL:	Yes. Well. I expect you have many things to attend to. Goodbye, Prime Minister.
	[ATTLEE *returns to his papers.* CARVEL *meets* VIOLET *and* ROSE *as he goes out and they come in.*]
CARVEL:	Best of luck to you, young lady. You'll need it.
ROSE:	Is it still hard to get a word out of him?
CARVEL:	It's like throwing sticks for a dog. All you get back from him is yup, yup, yup.
	[*exit* CARVEL.]
VIOLET:	He'll be so pleased to see you again, Rose. Don't expect him to show it too much though. That's not his way. You know that.
ROSE:	Doesn't sound as though he's changed much.
VIOLET:	Worse than ever, I'm afraid. It's being Prime Minister. He thinks every word he says could cause trouble. The fewer words he says, the better chance he's got. You'll be lucky to get three words together out of him.
ROSE:	What's the best subject to start with? Get him going a bit?
VIOLET:	Try cricket.
ROSE:	Cricket?
VIOLET:	You remember how he loves cricket. Clem, dear, a lovely surprise. The *Daily Herald* reporter is Rose. You remember lovely Rose, who taught you to make speeches, back in Limehouse. You thought you'd

	lost her to the Communists. But she's back in the Labour Party now.
ATTLEE:	Remember well.
VIOLET:	Rose, you don't mind if I sit in on this, do you? I might even be able to help, just a little.
ROSE:	Not at all, Mrs Attlee. Prime Minister. [*she looks slyly at* VIOLET.] I've taken a bet with someone that I can get more than three words together out of you.
ATTLEE:	You lose.
	[ATTLEE *allows himself the ghost of a smile.* ROSE *looks at* VIOLET, *who mouths "cricket."*]
ROSE:	I expect you were pleased to see Alec Bedser taking 11 wickets in the First Test against India, at Lord's?
ATTLEE:	Yes.
ROSE:	Oh, good. Well, now, Prime Minister, moving on from that….
ATTLEE:	First test he'd played in. Very talented player. Great addition to English cricket. He's got a twin brother, you know, Eric Bedser, useful bowler, useful bat as well. First full season of first-class cricket after the war. Pity the weather wasn't better. English cricket is coming back after the war, y'know. Remember last year, first year they played, Len Hutton and Cyril Washbrook walking out to open the batting for England on the first morning of the first victory test match against Australia. Quite a moment. Of course, strictly speaking, it wasn't an Australian national team, it was an Australian Services eleven, not everyone understands that. It wasn't an official test match for the ashes, you see. But a big moment all the same. The very first moment of first-class cricket in England since 1939.
ROSE:	That's very interesting. I wonder if we could move onto government policy now…
ATTLEE:	Best moment I could recall since 1938 when Wally Hammond reached his double century in the test match against Australia at Lord's.

ROSE:	Really?
ATTLEE:	And before that you have to go back to 1934. That was England's first win against Australia at Lord's since 1896, by an innings and 38 runs. Hedley Verity of Yorkshire took 8 for 43 in the second innings – and he got Don Bradman out for low scores in both inningses. Poor old Hedley Verity, he died serving in Italy during the war. So wasteful, war.
ROSE:	And of course, the war also leaves your government with a wrecked economy. Will that be an excuse for not carrying out your manifesto pledges? Can we be sure your government won't betray its people, as previous Labour governments have done?
ATTLEE:	Used to play cricket at Haileybury, y'know.
ROSE:	Hedley Verity did?
ATTLEE:	No, I did. Never much good though. There were some fine cricketers there. Also there are three old Haileyburians in the Parliamentary Labour Party now. And the Arts Council has a majority of Old Haileyburians. This is a somewhat unusual occurrence.
ROSE:	Can I ask you about your attitude to the atom bomb?
ATTLEE:	As is the number of bishops that come from my old Oxford College, which was University College. I was surprised to find the other day how many bishops are former Univ men. I can tell you the number exactly.
ROSE:	I'd be quite satisfied with an approximation.
ATTLEE:	I dislike approximations. Like my cabinet ministers to be exact when they report. Choosing a cabinet is very like choosing a cricket eleven.
ROSE:	Is it really?
ATTLEE:	Very. You have to have your big hitters, chaps who will knock the opposition for six.
	[NYE BEVAN *bounds into the room, excited.*]
NYE:	Clem. Wonderful news...

	[VIOLET *holds up her hand to silence* NYE.]
ATTLEE:	But your big hitters might not have the staying power. They'll knock up centuries, like Wally Hammond, you see, but then one day they'll over-reach themselves, out first ball. So you have to have your solid workhorses. Chaps who will plug away.
	[*enter* MORRISON.]
MORRISON:	Clem, I need to talk to you.
ATTLEE:	Then you've got to have your seam bowlers, your fast bowlers, your medium fast bowlers.
MORRISON:	Clem, I need a word.
VIOLET:	Not yet.
MORRISON:	What's he doing that's so important?
VIOLET:	Breathing.
MORRISON:	What do you mean, breathing?
VIOLET:	He's coming up for air.
ATTLEE:	My prep school was run by two clergymen who knew a lot about cricket. Prep school was called Northaw House. They taught you a lot about cricket. Not much else. Curious fact about Northaw. The only three Members of Parliament who had been at Northaw all held government office in 1931.
ROSE:	[*with irony.*] How very interesting.
ATTLEE:	One in the Labour government before the summer, that was me, and the other two in the National government after the summer. A somewhat remarkable fact.
ROSE:	Extremely.
ATTLEE:	I collect facts. Good for the memory. I can remem-ber the names of all the boys in my class at Northaw when I was eleven.
VIOLET:	He really can, you know.
ROSE:	I'm happy to take it on trust.
ATTLEE:	Arbuthnot, Attlee, Bailey, Biggins, Blackstone,

NYE:	He's not going to give us the lot, is he?
ATTLEE:	Diamond, Fortescue, Franklin, Harley, Jowitt, Mallory Major, Montmorency Minor, Norris, Taylor, Turnbull, Tyrrhitt-Drake,
MORRISON:	For Heaven's sake.
ATTLEE:	Utley, Walton, Wells, Wiley, Wilson.
MORRISON:	That's all, surely?
ATTLEE:	Zacharias.
MORRISON:	That must be all.
ATTLEE:	Very small classes at Northaw. Yes, Nye?
NYE:	Clem, I've done a deal with the British Medical Association. We can go ahead with the National Health Service bill. The doctors don't like it, but they won't try to wreck it.
MORRISON:	What did you do?
NYE:	I stuffed their mouths with gold.
ATTLEE:	Good work. Check with Chancellor?
NYE:	Hugh Dalton says he can do it if you don't mind a big hike in income tax. They'll tell us we're attacking the wealth creators. It's rubbish of course. The rich don't create wealth. They just shift wealth. Mostly towards themselves. They'll howl. Press will support them.
ATTLEE:	Worth it. Herbert?
MORRISON:	We can go ahead with rail nationalisation. I've reached agreement on compensation with the owners. Won't be cheap. But it'll stop the owners making a killing out of a natural monopoly. No one will ever be so stupid as to privatise them again.
ATTLEE:	Good work. Check with Chancellor?
MORRISON:	Hugh Dalton says he's sick of all of us coming to him for money, and yes he'll find it. Means another hike in tax. On top of Nye's hike. And what Ellen wants for schools. And Jim Griffiths wants for unemployment pay. Higher taxes than Britain's ever had

	before. You'll have to defend that, Clem.
ATTLEE:	Decent society doesn't come cheap. That it?
NYE:	Yes, what I'll do now, you see, is...
ATTLEE:	Good show.
MORRISON:	I think he wants us to leave now.
NYE:	Unless you've got any fascinating facts about test cricket to offer him.

[NYE *and* MORRISON *go out.*]

ROSE:	That's the last two pieces in the jigsaw, isn't it? This is a big moment, isn't it, Mr Attlee? I'm so pleased I was here to see it. How do you feel?
ATTLEE:	Content.
ROSE:	And you almost didn't go into politics. You hated public speaking so much.
ATTLEE:	Yes.
ROSE:	I helped teach you.
ATTLEE:	Quite.
ROSE:	Can I ask...
ATTLEE:	Few things I need to look at.
VIOLET:	Come on, Rose, you and I will go and see Mr Williams and get a quote sorted out. Mr Williams will give you a much better quote from Clem than anything Clem will actually say. Come on, dear, I'm dying to hear how the family is.
ROSE:	Goodbye, Mr Attlee. Major Attlee. It was a pleasure seeing you again, Major Attlee. Really.
ATTLEE:	For me too.

[*exit* VIOLET *and* ROSE *as* ATTLEE *sits down with a pen and paper.*

ATTLEE *writes. When he has finished, he puts his pen down, clears his throat, and begins to speak.*]

| ATTLEE: | Tomorrow there will come into operation the most comprehensive system of social security ever introduced into any country. When I first went to |

work in East London, the only provision for the citizen unable to work through sickness, unemployment or old age was that given by the Poor Law. The Poor Law was designed to be, and indeed was, the last refuge of the destitute. Today's four new Acts of Parliament are based on a new principle: that we must combine together to meet contingencies with which we cannot cope as individual citizens. The question is asked: can we afford it? Supposing the answer is no, what does that mean? It means that the sum total of the goods produced and the services rendered by the people of this country is not sufficient to provide for all our people at all times, in sickness, in health, in youth and in age, the very modest standard of life which these Acts guarantee.

LIGHTS DOWN ON ATTLEE.

LIGHTS UP ON VIOLET.

VIOLET: 5 July 1948. The day Clem's government created the welfare state. It couldn't get better than that, and of course it didn't. Three years later Labour was out, and Winston scraped back in. Eventually Clem retired. I was a lot younger than him, and he worried that he'd die and not leave enough money for me to live comfortably. A former Prime Minister can't very well scratch around trying to make money, can he? It wouldn't be decent. Well, it didn't matter in the end, because I died first, so that was all right. And the day I died, he burned all the letters he'd ever sent to me, every last one. Clem wouldn't want strangers reading them and putting them in books. He burned some of his poems, too. But this one survived, because he put it in a letter to his brother Tom, they day they made Clem an Earl.

[*enter* ATTLEE.]

ATTLEE: Few thought he was even a starter
There were many who thought themselves smarter

But he ended PM
CH and OM
An Earl and a Knight of the Garter

www.ingramcontent.com/pod-product-compliance
Lightning Source LLC
LaVergne TN
LVHW021119080426
835509LV00021B/3446